She Persisted

Around the World

13 Women Who Changed History

"One of our goals is that people in society will accept that girls play soccer."

"The more I did, the more I could do, the more I wanted to do."

"I don't really know why I care so much. I just have something inside me that tells me that there is a problem."

"When I proposed changing the laws before, the fanatics staged demonstrations against me . . ."

"We are tired of having a 'sphere' doled out to us, and of being told that anything outside that sphere is 'unwomanly.'"

"We do not need magic to transform our world; we carry all the power we need inside ourselves already."

"We will continue to fight for reform."

"I don't study to know more but to ignore less."

"One child, one teacher, one book and one pen can change the world."

"I don't try to be anyone else."

"However long we live, life is short, so I work."

"We must be ourselves at all risks."

"Nothing in life is to be feared, it is only to be understood."

"I didn't realize a thing like this could happen in Nova Scotia—or in any other part of Canada."

"At first the threads seemed so tangled and broken, but I am beginning to think that life may have a pattern after all."

"While I watch other dancers do the same roles I do, I don't try to be anyone else."

Written by
Chelsea Clinton

Illustrated by
Alexandra Boiger

PHILOMEL BOOKS

Philomel Books
an imprint of Penguin Random House LLC
375 Hudson Street
New York, NY 10014

Library of Congress Cataloging-in-Publication Data is available upon request.

Manufactured in the United States of America.
ISBN 9780525516996
10 9 8 7 6 5 4 3 2 1

Edited by Jill Santopolo.
Design by Ellice M. Lee.
Text set in ITC Kennerley.
The art was done in watercolor and ink on Fabriano paper, then edited in Photoshop.

In memory of my grandmother Dorothy,
whose persistence, curiosity and love
inspire me every day. —C.C.

To my daughter, Vanessa, and to
children everywhere around
this precious globe. —A.B.

She Persisted

It's not always easy being a girl—anywhere in the world. It's especially challenging in some places. There are countries where it's hard for girls to go to school and where women need their husbands' permission to get a passport or even to leave the house. And all over the world, girls are more likely to be told to be quiet, to sit down, to have smaller dreams.

Don't listen to those voices. These thirteen women from across the world didn't.

They persisted.

At the time

SOR JUANA INÉS DE LA CRUZ

was growing up in Mexico, most girls did not go to school.
After reading and studying on her own, Juana Inés asked
her family if she could disguise herself as a boy so she
could go to university; they said no. **She persisted**,
finding tutors who didn't mind teaching a girl, and then
became a nun in part so that she could focus on her
studies and her writing. Sor Juana Inés' poems and plays
are still celebrated today and her *Respuesta a Sor Filotea
de la Cruz* was the first published argument for a woman's
right to education in the Americas.

"I don't study to know more but to ignore less."

Respuesta a Sor Filotea de la Cruz

Although CAROLINE HERSCHEL's mother didn't think girls should be educated, her father taught her alongside her brothers. But after typhus left Caroline permanently stunted at just over four feet tall, both parents thought her only future was to be a servant. She persisted, leaving her native Germany to live in England with her brother William, who supported her efforts to further educate herself, including in math and astronomy. Together, they studied the night sky, and on her own, Caroline became the first woman to discover a comet. Today, several of the comets she found bear her name.

"However long we live, life is short, so I work."

When KATE SHEPPARD began traveling throughout New Zealand, saying that women deserved voting rights, many men believed that women should avoid "meddling in masculine concerns." When Kate first tried to get Parliament to give women the right to vote, they didn't listen, even though she brought them many petitions that thousands of women had signed. Still, **she persisted**, and in 1893, New Zealand became the first country to grant all women—including indigenous Maori women—the right to vote.

"We are tired of having a 'sphere' doled out to us,
and of being told that anything outside that sphere is
'unwomanly.' . . . We must be ourselves at all risks."

Growing up in Poland, MARIE CURIE knew that because she was a girl, she would have to leave her country to go to college. **She persisted,** moving to France to pursue her dream of being a scientist. Her work in radioactivity—the way that some materials give off energy—led to her becoming the first woman awarded a Nobel Prize (in Physics). A few years later, she discovered two new elements, one of which she named polonium after her home country. For that work, she won her second Nobel Prize (in Chemistry). She was the first person in the world—man or woman—to receive two Nobel Prizes.

$[Xe] 4f^{14} 5d^{10} 6s^2 6p^4$

$[Rn] 7s^2$

"Nothing in life is to be feared, it is only to be understood."

When VIOLA DESMOND was on a
business trip, her car broke down, so she decided to
go to the movies while she waited for it to be fixed.
But Viola didn't know that in the town she was
visiting, only white Canadians were allowed to sit
on the movie theater's main floor. When Viola was
asked to leave, **she persisted** in saying that it
was her right to sit wherever she wanted. Viola was
arrested and spent the night in jail. Her decision to
fight the charges against her helped start the modern
civil rights movement in Canada.

"I didn't realize a thing like this could happen in Nova Scotia— or in any other part of Canada."

While working in India as a young doctor focused on caring for women, MARY VERGHESE was in a terrible car crash and lost the use of her legs. Rather than quit medicine, **she persisted** and shifted her work to the kind of care she could give patients from her wheelchair just as well as anyone could standing up. She focused on rehabilitation, working with people who had also lost the use of their legs or faced other challenges after accidents or illnesses. Mary founded the first functional rehabilitation center in India; it still helps patients today.

"At first the threads seemed so tangled
and broken, but I am beginning to think
that life may have a pattern after all."

After going to law school, AISHA RATEB hoped
to become a judge in Egypt. But the then prime minister
told Aisha that she couldn't because a female judge
would be against the traditions of society.
She persisted in doing important
legal work, helping to write a new
constitution for Egypt, crafting
new rules to protect women
and people with disabilities,
and serving as Egypt's first
female ambassador. More
than fifty years after Aisha
was told no, the first woman
was appointed to Egypt's highest
court, thanks, in part, to Aisha.

As the first woman in East and Central Africa to earn a doctorate degree and become a professor at the University of Nairobi, WANGARI MAATHAI made two of her dreams come true. Still, she wanted to do more. Horrified by how many trees had been cut down across Kenya, Wangari started to plant trees. **She persisted** in getting family, friends, students and even strangers to help plant more trees and to respect the environment. She also worked hard to protect and defend the rights of everyone in Kenya. Wangari was the first African woman awarded the Nobel Peace Prize; her legacy includes the more than 50 million trees her Green Belt Movement has planted.

"I don't really know why I care so much.
I just have something inside me
that tells me that there is a problem,
and I have got to do something about it."

As a little girl in the United Kingdom, **JOANNE ROWLING** knew she wanted to be a writer. After university, she spent years creating the Harry Potter world—while also working full-time. Even though many publishers rejected her first book, **she persisted**. The publisher she finally found worried that boy readers might not want to read a book featuring a boy wizard written by a woman, and asked Joanne to publish as J.K.—it sounded less female. Today, the Harry Potter series is the best-selling book series in history, with more than 400 million books in print in eighty languages, and its author is famous as the woman who brought more magic into the world.

"We do not
need magic
to transform our
world; we carry all
the power we need
inside ourselves
already."

When Sisleide "SISSI" Lima do Amor was young, it was against the law for girls to play soccer in Brazil. But Sissi wanted to play, even if she got in trouble. So, **she persisted**, first in secret, turning other toys into soccer balls and practicing whenever she could. Eventually, Sissi's parents got her a soccer ball. When she was fourteen, two years after Brazil made it legal for girls to play soccer, Sissi started playing professionally and then joined the first Brazilian women's national soccer team. At the height of her career, Sissi was called the "Queen of Brazilian football" and today is credited with inspiring a generation of Brazilian girls to be unafraid to take the field.

"One of our goals is that people in society will accept that girls play soccer."

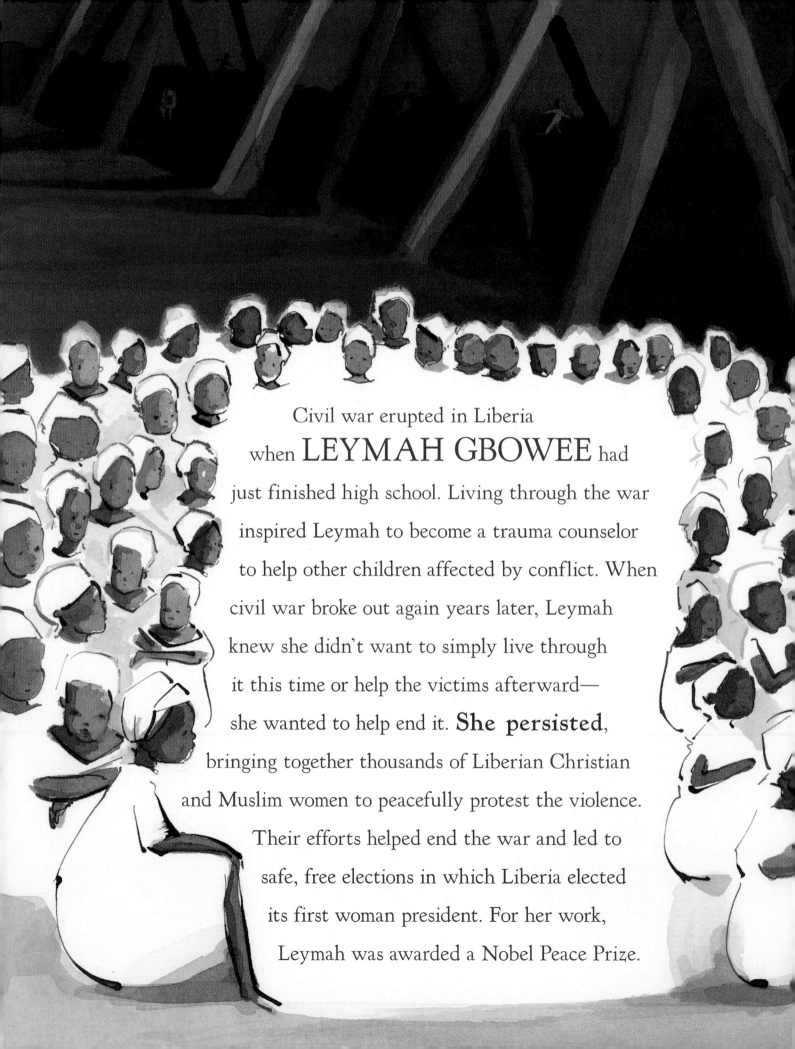

Civil war erupted in Liberia
when LEYMAH GBOWEE had
just finished high school. Living through the war
inspired Leymah to become a trauma counselor
to help other children affected by conflict. When
civil war broke out again years later, Leymah
knew she didn't want to simply live through
it this time or help the victims afterward—
she wanted to help end it. **She persisted**,
bringing together thousands of Liberian Christian
and Muslim women to peacefully protest the violence.
Their efforts helped end the war and led to
safe, free elections in which Liberia elected
its first woman president. For her work,
Leymah was awarded a Nobel Peace Prize.

"One of our goals is that people in society will accept that girls play soccer."

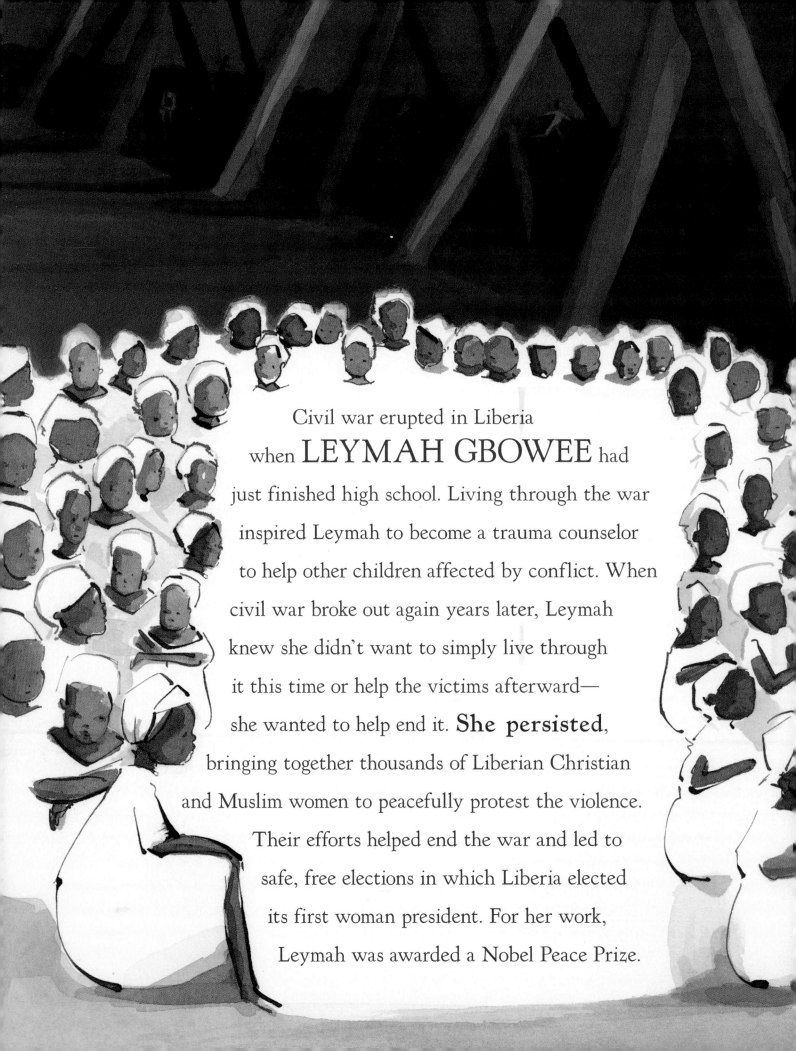

Civil war erupted in Liberia when **LEYMAH GBOWEE** had just finished high school. Living through the war inspired Leymah to become a trauma counselor to help other children affected by conflict. When civil war broke out again years later, Leymah knew she didn't want to simply live through it this time or help the victims afterward— she wanted to help end it. **She persisted**, bringing together thousands of Liberian Christian and Muslim women to peacefully protest the violence. Their efforts helped end the war and led to safe, free elections in which Liberia elected its first woman president. For her work, Leymah was awarded a Nobel Peace Prize.

"The more I did, the more I could do,
the more I wanted to do, the more I saw needed to be done."

When
she was
growing up in
China, YUAN
YUAN TAN's
father did not want his daughter
to take ballet. **She persisted** in
convincing him that being a dancer was
her destiny. Finally, her father said that he
would decide Yuan Yuan's fate with a coin toss.
If the coin landed on heads, she could pursue ballet.

If the coin landed on tails, she couldn't.

Yuan Yuan won the coin toss. She went on
to become among the most famous Chinese
ballerinas of all time, winning many awards,
dancing around the world and becoming the
youngest principal dancer ever at the San
Francisco Ballet, where she still performs today.

"While I watch other dancers do the same roles I do, I don't try to be anyone else."

When MALALA YOUSAFZAI
was eleven, she began writing about how much
she wanted to get an education, even though some
people in her native Pakistan thought girls shouldn't
go to school. Malala was threatened many times,
but she persisted in writing about her dreams
for herself and girls everywhere. When Malala was
fifteen, a man boarded her school bus and shot her,
targeting her because of her courage in standing up
for girls' right to go to school. Even after she was
hurt, Malala didn't give up. She is the youngest-ever
Nobel Peace Prize winner and still works hard in the
hope that one day every child will be able to go to
school—all while she herself is still in school.

"One child, one teacher, one book
and one pen can change the world."

So, speak up, rise up, dream big.
These women did that and more.

POETS

DOCTORS
HEAL

FOREST
Preservation

They persisted and so should you.